Learning God's Love Language

Personal Hebrew Word Study

WORKBOOK

Learning God's Love Language Workbook was originally published as Beyond the Hebrew Lexicon Manual/Workbook in 2015.

All Bible quotations are from the One New Man Bible

Learning God's Love Language: Personal Hebrew Word Study Workbook
Chaim Bentorah

Cover and Interior Page design by True Potential, Inc.

ISBN: 9781943852932 (paperback)

ISBN: 9781943852949 (ebook)

Library of Congress Control Number:

True Potential, Inc.

PO Box 904, Travelers Rest, SC 29690

www.truepotentialmedia.com

Printed in the United States of America.

TABLE OF CONTENTS

INTRODUCTION

There is an old proverb, *"Give a man a fish and you feed him for a day; teach a man to fish, and you feed him for a lifetime."* This comes from an even older proverb; *"It is more worthwhile to teach someone to do something than to do it for him."*

My books have been feeding Christians for a day, that is, I have been doing Hebrew word studies every day for my former students that I send out via e-mail and post online. It is time that we move forward with the resources that are available to us through 21st-century technology. I can now teach you *to fish,* to do your own word studies, so you will be fed for a lifetime.

As we've moved well into the 21st century, we are flooded by modern media giving us our daily meal. If you are not satisfied with getting just the milk of the Word and you want the real meat of the Word, and you have no Bible college or seminary training, all you need to do today is push a button to receive any information you could possibly want. You can go to the internet, television, purchase DVD's, CD's, podcasts, webinars, conferences and the many other opportunities to discover the depths of God's Word in ways that were never available to our fathers.

Yet, you are still being fed. You are still being given someone else's knowledge. You are still being led by someone who managed to build a platform, can wave credentials, or who claims to have more personal spiritual insight than you; encouraging you to believe their spin on God's Word.

The greatest teacher of God's Word is the Holy Spirit, that member of the Godhead who desires a personal relationship with you and longs to speak a personal message to you.

Let us embrace our modern world and its technology. Let us embrace the great advances in the sciences of linguistics, archaeology and other disciplines. Take in as much knowledge as you can, lay it before the Holy Spirit and say, "Ok, you choose what is right for me. You choose which translation is the one you want to use to speak to me."

A hundred years ago most people had few resources they could turn to when they found a passage of Scripture difficult to understand. They could go to their pastor and ask. He may have been to seminary, may have studied Greek and Hebrew so you would have assumed he would know the answers. You would never question his answer, just as you would never question the diagnosis of your family physician.

Today, however, the family physician is no longer the final authority on your affliction or your cure. He is a gateway to a specialist or diagnostic testing's. Most often he would even encourage you to seek a second opinion. When he sends you to a specialist or for a diagnostic test he is saying, "I don't know, I need more information."

If you need legal advice, many times an attorney will recommend another attorney who specializes in the particular field in which you need assistance. You wouldn't go to a real estate attorney with a tax issue. You would go to an attorney who is focused on tax law.

Unfortunately, a lot of organized religion has been a little slow to embrace the fact that there now exists a tremendous explosion of knowledge in linguistics, archaeology, history, sociology, etc. which has shed new light on Scripture. So much, that no one pastor could apply all of this knowledge at the moment someone asks a question about a challenging passage of Scripture. Pastor's need to stop saying, "Well, the answer is," or "our church teaches…" and start saying, "Give me a few days to research it, and I will get back with you."

Yet, that Pastor is going to do what you are fully capable of doing yourself, and that is going to your computer and looking up your question online. But you say, "My pastor has studied Greek and Hebrew, he knows much more than I do."

All I can say is that I taught Hebrew to many, many future pastors in Bible College; some who even took my advanced Hebrew classes. I would be surprised to discover if any of them today are actually studying God's Word in Hebrew on a daily basis. The vast majority do what you can easily do on your own, they go to their computers, look up the passage and read all the commentaries and studies that have been done on a particular passage and report back to you with a learned answer that fits his doctrinal position.

You are allowing your pastor to *give you a fish,* which I do not at all condemn. We need, however, to face reality; most American Christians are just too lazy to fish for themselves, to study God's Word, to find their own answers. They need their pastors to keep feeding them, or they starve to death spiritually.

I regularly receive mail from people who read my books and say that they are tired of hearing the same thing over and over in church; they want some depth to God's Word, they want some meat. They become disgusted with their church and pastor and leave. That is a big mistake and a tragedy. The very people who could add a sense of maturity in the church, who could begin to disciple and mentor younger believers get disgusted with their pastor because he spends all his time feeding babies and ignoring them.

I once knew a guy from a family of twelve brothers and sisters. I asked how his mother was able to care for them all. He said that the older children helped to care for the younger children. When a church grows, the mature saints need to care for the younger saints, not drop out because they are not getting the attention that the younger saints need and deserve from their pastors.

Pastors have their hands full just feeding the milk of the Word to new Christians. It's time that mature Christians start studying God's Word themselves, grow up and take their place in the family and help care for the younger saints.

As far as receiving the meat of God's Word, there is absolutely no reason you cannot learn to fish for yourself. The resources are out there and available. This manual is merely a guide to help you utilize those resources as you study God's Word in the original Hebrew. All you need are the six lessons in this workbook to be on your way to doing Hebrew word studies at a depth on par with my advanced Hebrew students, maybe even better, thanks to the technological tools we have today, using your computer and accessing the internet.

The premise of this study is that it is the Holy Spirit is the ultimate teacher. It is the Holy Spirit who will lead and guide you into all truth. If you do not believe that, if you feel you can only be taught the depths of God's Word from a human teacher or organization, then this book may be of little value. The Holy Spirit wants to speak to you just as much as he does to any Hebrew scholar; is He not capable of getting His message to you personally? Of course, He is.

Before you begin I must remind you of Jeremiah 29:13 "And you will seek Me and find Me, when you will search for me with your heart."

This workbook is not promoting any specific doctrine, theology or dogma, it is only providing a tool to aid you as you seek and search for God with all your heart.

LESSON 1

THE HISTORY OF THE HEBREW ALPHABET

LESSON 1
THE HISTORY OF
THE HEBREW ALPHABET

First, let me introduce you the Hebrew Alphabet. This workbook will not teach you the pronunciation for each letter as this is not a course in learning to speak Hebrew. A YouTube search for "Hebrew Alphabet" will turn up several videos that can teach the pronunciation of Hebrew letters.

This workbook will not demonstrate how to write Hebrew letters. Again, the internet contains resources that can explain how to write Hebrew letters.

This workbook will provide the Hebrew Alphabet as a handy resource as you will be using this alphabet often. It will be beneficial to memorize the Hebrew alphabet in its proper order, as this will be helpful when you begin looking for these words in your Hebrew lexicon. The Hebrew lexicon is a dictionary of Hebrew words. You look up a Hebrew word in a Hebrew lexicon just as you would an English word in an English dictionary, each word being in alphabetical order.

The Alphabet this workbook describes is in what is called the Square Script or the Assyrian Script. The Hebrew borrowed some different scripts during its evolutionary process.

The Ugaritic, which is related to the Hebrew, is in cuneiform, which you may have seen in museums on clay tablets. The cuneiform alphabet is made up of a series of triangles and lines.

The Hebrew also borrowed a script from the Phoenicians, who were merchants and needed a form of written communication to carry on their business. This is also referred to as the Canaanite Script. Some have called this the "Ancient Hebrew Script," which is misleading, as it was a common script in the Canaanite region and Hebrew was just one of many languages that used it. This script was heavily influenced by pagan cultures, which may have prompted Ezra and his scribes to develop a script that was solely indigenous to the Hebrew language. This became known as the Assyrian Script, as it was developed during the Jewish captivity in Assyria. It is more popularly known as the Square Script.

There are some who seek to use the pictures of the Canaanite Script to come to a deeper understanding of a Hebrew word. Linguistically there might be some value, although most consider the application of the pictures to develop a meaning for a word to be merely *snake oil.* My concern is that those who rely on the Canaanite script are using pagan symbols to describe our relationship with God. For instance, the Aleph in the Canaanite Script is an ox's head. In ancient times an ox and a bull were considered the same animal, and it is more than likely a bull's head, which was the symbol of the Egyptian god Apis. The Hebrews exchanged the picture of a bull's head for the Square Script א. The diagonal line is the letter Vav and the two dots on either side of the line are Yods. It spells out ייו which is an abbreviated form of the name of God.

In my book *Learning God's Love Language Personal Hebrew Word Study* you will find an in-depth study of these letters, however, let me just introduce them to you.

LETTER		FINAL FORM	NUMERICAL VALUE
ALEPH	א		1
BETH	ב		2
GIMMEL	ג		3
DALET	ד		4
HEI	ה		5
VAV	ו		6
ZAYIN	ז		7
CHETH	ח		8
TETH	ט		9
YOD	י		10
KAP	כ	ך	20
LAMED	ל		30
MEM	מ	ם	40
NUN	נ	ן	50
SAMEK	ס		60
AYIN	ע		70
PEI	פ	ף	80
SADE	צ	ץ	90
QOP	ק		100
RESH	ר		200
SHIN, SINE	ש ש		300
TAW	ת		400

You will notice under *final form* I have a symbol for five of the letters. That particular symbol is used when the letter happens to be the last letter in a word. The reason to use a different symbol when it is the last letter is that in the original Hebrew there were no spaces between words as we have today. You did not know where a word ended or where it began unless you were really familiar with the language. The final form of a letter helped the reader know when one word has ended and when the next word begins.

Also, you will notice in the final column a number. This is unlike English, which has separate numeric symbols for numbers. The letters also moonlight as numbers as well, with each letter representing a number. We will discuss this further in Lesson Four.

At this point, I would encourage you to visit YouTube and view some videos on speaking and writing the Hebrew Alphabet. Write the Alphabet out and maybe even try to memorize the Alphabet, although this is not really necessary. Hopefully, you will learn the Hebrew Alphabet through using it.

QUESTIONS

1. How many letters are there in the Hebrew Alphabet?

2. Which Hebrew Script is in use today?

    a. Canaanite

    b. Ancient Hebrew

    c. Square

    d. Phoenician

3. Why is the Square Script sometimes called the Assyrian Script?

4. What is one possible reason the Square Script was introduced?

5. It is believed by some that a biblical character introduced the Square Script. Who was this Biblical character?

6. What is one reason for memorizing the Hebrew alphabet to aid you in doing a Hebrew word study?

7. What is one reason why certain Hebrew letters have a final form?

8. What is the number 30 in Hebrew?

9. In the Phoenician Script what did the Aleph represent?

10. In the Square Script what does the Aleph represent?

ANSWERS

1. 22

2. Square

3. It was developed during the Assyrian captivity

4. The Canaanite Script was built on pagan symbols

5. Ezra

6. Hebrew words in a lexicon are in alphabetical order

7. The original Hebrew had no spaces between words

8. Lamed ל

9. The god Apis

10. The God Jehovah

LESSON II

FINDING HEBREW WORDS

LESSON 2
FINDING HEBREW WORDS

The Interlinear

So let's say you are reading Psalms 23:1 and you come across the word *shepherd*. Your spirit is quickened, and you feel that there must be more to this word *shepherd* than meets the eye. You realize that this was originally written in Hebrew and you wonder what the Hebrew word is for *"shepherd."*

There are many ways to find out. The most common is to look up the word in Strong's Concordance. You may have a Bible dictionary and can look up the word there.

Or you can go online, type Psalms 23:1 into your search engine and find results from *Bible Hub* and *Study Light* which will provide a storehouse of information. These sites offer Psalms 23:1 in many English translations and commentaries, as well as links to an *Interlinear,* which gives the Hebrew word with an English equivalent above or beneath that Hebrew word. You will also find on the menu at the top of these pages, along with the various parallel English translations, a tab, which says *Interlinear.* Clicking on that tab, takes you to a page that will give Psalms 23:1 as found in the Interlinear. Let's focus on the word *shepherd.* This is what you would find on the Interlinear:

7462 [e]

ro i

רֹעִי

[is] my shepherd

Verb

Look at the phrase *(is) my shepherd,* and you will find that above the English phrase is רֹעִי, the Hebrew word for *(is) my shepherd.* Above that is the word *ro i* which is the transliteration of the word or how you would pronounce it in English. The word is spelled Resh ר which makes the sound of an *R*, Ayin ע which has no sound; it is a silent letter, and Yod י which in this case is used as a vowel and makes the sound of an *i*. Now keep in mind that Hebrew is read from right to left, not left to right as in English, so the word starts with the Resh ר. Note below the word *shepherd* is the word *Verb*. Now we know the word shepherd is a noun, but you will notice that the word *is* in brackets *[is]*. That is because there is no verb in that sentence. In English, we cannot have a sentence without a verb, but in Hebrew, you can have a sentence without a verb so what we do is attach a linking verb, in this case, the verb *is,* to the direct object which is the word *shepherd*. The letter *i* at the end of the word *roi* רעי is really the first person personal pronoun *my*. In Hebrew, a word has prefixes and suffixes to indicate articles, prepositions, number, gender, and pronouns.

This is where we get into grammar. This is the reason so many students give up on learning Hebrew or dropping out of a Hebrew class, as many did when I taught Hebrew in Bible College. There were some who even failed their college class in Hebrew as they just could not discipline themselves to memorize all the declensions or grammatical pointings.

I will show you further on in this chapter how you can avoid all this memorization and be able to identify each suffix and prefix like an advanced Hebrew student, without taking a single Hebrew class.

The number above the transliterated word *roi,* 7462, is the corresponding number in Strong's Concordance, which you may or may not use. If you are using Bible Hub or Study Light you will most likely use their online lexicon, which gives more detail than Strong's Concordance. Strong's Concordance, however, is a valuable resource for making a quick reference.

So now we have the Hebrew word for *shepherd roi* רעי that is really three words in English, *"is my shepherd."* Another important rule to remember is that every word in Hebrew has a three-letter root or what is called a *triliteral root*. There are only about 7,500 words in Classical Hebrew, compared to a 1,025,109 (and still counting) words in modern English. There are a similar number of words in Modern Hebrew or Israeli Hebrew.

There is an ongoing debate over whether Israeli Hebrew is a Semitic language at all, and whether it is really a direct continuation of the Classical or Biblical Hebrew. Israeli Hebrew is considered by some to be just a relexified Yiddish which is a combination of Hebrew and German with Israeli Hebrew. Many linguists feel Modern Israeli Hebrew is just a hybrid of Polish, Russian, German, English, Latin, and Arabic rooted in Classical or Biblical Hebrew. In other words, if you are seeking to learn Hebrew to study the Bible, be careful that you understand just what type of Hebrew course you sign up for. If you wish to speak Hebrew, then seek a class that teaches Israeli Hebrew. If you wish to learn ceremonial Hebrew as you would find in a synagogue, then learn that Hebrew in a synagogue, but keep in mind there are many different ways in which Hebrew words can be pronounced and it will vary from teacher to teacher.

Hebrew Lexicons

For the sake of simplicity, let us just call a lexicon a dictionary. You look up a word as you would look up a word in your English dictionary and find the part of speech, gender, number, and its various usages and definitions.

In the English dictionary, the words are all in alphabetical order, and you look up the word according to the English alphabet. The same is true for the Hebrew lexicon only the words are in alphabetical order according to the Hebrew Alphabet, not the English Alphabet. I mean fair is fair, right?

The standard and most comprehensive Hebrew lexicon is The Brown-Driver-Briggs Hebrew and English Lexicon published by Hendrickson Publishers. The problem with this lexicon, however, is the word you will find in your interlinear may not be the word you are going to look up. Remember, I said that all Hebrew words are built on a three-letter root word. For instance, you have the word for *king melek* מלך which is your three letter root word Mem מ, Lamed ל and Final Kap ך. You will be able to look that word up in the Brown-Driver-Briggs Lexicon (BDB) without any problem, just look it up under words starting with Mem מ. However, more often than not that word will have a prefix before it. You may see it as *lamelek* למלך (to the king) or you may find it as *kamelek* (like a king) כמלך. If you try to look the word up under the Lamed ל or the Kap כ you won't find it. The BDB only lists the words in their root form. If you have not studied Hebrew for two or three years and memorized all the prefixes and suffixes you will not know if the three letter root word in *lamelek* למלך (to a king) is Lamed ל, Mem מ, and Lamed ל or Mem מ, Lamed ל, and Final Kap ך. Or in the case of *kamelek* כמלך if the root word is Kap כ, Mem מ, Lamed ל or Mem מ, Lamed ל, Final Kap ך.

Of course, these days you can get around this by looking up the word in the BDB online, which is found on www.studylight.org. Just type the English word "king" into your search book, and there you are. Also, the more recent editions of the BDB is coded with the Strong's Concordance number which will take you right to the word, but you must first look it up in your Strong's Concordance.

Another way to avoid the root word in order to look up a Hebrew word is to download a convenient little APP that you can find under Hebrew Bible by Zev Clementson. This APP will give you the Hebrew Bible in the left column and the English version in the right column. Place your finger over the Hebrew word in the Hebrew Bible and suddenly there appears the BDB, right on the page for the word you are looking up. This is a wonderful tool that I use all the time.

Of course, if you are old-fashioned, you can go to a bookstore and impress the clerk by purchasing a copy of the BDB, or your can order the print version online. I would also encourage you to purchase a Strong's Concordance as well, so you have the code to look up a word in the BDB without figuring out what the root word would be.

As I said, the BDB is the most comprehensive lexicon tracing a word through its Semitic origins. When you look up a word in the BDB you may find an abbreviation like Ak, this tells you its use in the Akkadian language. You may see As. for Assyrian, Ar. for Arabic, Syr. for Syriac (Aramaic), Skr. for Sanskrit, Sum for Sumerian or Ph. for Phoenician. Pay close attention to these abbreviations for they are guiding you to the word's Semitic root.

Keep in mind that Hebrew belongs to a group of languages known as Semitic languages. Just as English is a European language which has borrowed its alphabet and many words for other European languages so too did Hebrew borrow many words from other Semitic languages, as sometimes you may find this etymology, that is tracing a word to its Semitic origins to help clarify or give you a greater depth of meaning.

For instance, you have the word *sarav* סרב, which means a rebel. Your BDB will tell you that this is a loan word from the Aramaic meaning to *tell lies*. This tells you something about a rebel, that they are liars. Now let's take a look at a verse that contains sarav סרב. Ezekiel 2:6 "And you, son of man, Do not be in awe of them! Do not be in awe of their words! You are among *briers* and thorns and you live among scorpions. Do not be in awe of their words! Do not be dismayed at their looks! They are a rebellious house."

You may ask, "What does it mean, "You are among *briers* and thorns"? The word for *briers* is *sarav* סרב. By looking that word up in your BDB you find that the prophet is really refer- ring to rebels. By tracing its Semitic root to an Aramaic word, thanks to BDB, you discover something more specific, these *briers* are not only *rebels*, but also *liars*.

There is another Lexicon that, initially, I would not allow my students to use because I felt it was cheating. This is called the Analytical Hebrew and Chaldee Lexicon by Benjamin David- son also published by Hendricks Publishers. Every word in the Hebrew Bible is listed in this lexicon. You merely look the word up as you find it in your Hebrew Bible and look it up like you look up a word in the dictionary.

Let's go back to our word for *king* and say you found the word lemeleke למלך. I would like to point out at this juncture that under the Hebrew letters you will find little dots and dashes such as לְ כְּ. These are vowels. In the original Hebrew, there were no vowels. Four consonants known as the weak consonants worked part-time as vowels Aleph א, Hei ה, Vav ו and Yod י.

Seven hundred years after Christ, a Jewish sect of scribes known as the Masoretes developed a system of diacritical symbols call niqqud (apply points) to create a system of vowels to preserve the proper vowel sounds. These pointings not only served to standardize the pro- nunciation of Hebrew words but also were used to enhance one's understanding of Hebrew grammar. These vowel pointings were not in the original inspired text of the Hebrew Bible. However, they do serve to help narrow down the particular word you are searching for when looking it up in your Analytical Lexicon. So be sure the word you find in your Analytical Lexicon matches the one you find in your Hebrew text. However, for the sake of simplicity, in this workbook, I will only use the consonants for illustration.

When you look up the word kemeleke כמלך in your Analytical Lexicon which you will find at the top left-hand corner of page 383 this following line:

כמלך pref. כ (noun masc. sing. suff. מלכי) , d.6a מלך

The כמלך is the word that you found in your interlinear, it will, of course have vowel point- ings. The word *pref.* is the abbreviation for prefix showing you that the Kap כ is a preposition. This is the prepositions *as* or *like*. This is unimportant in your word study, as any English translation of the Bible will express the preposition in English for you. So I would not worry too much about that. The same thing for the *noun masc. sing.* which I am sure you realize means noun masculine singular. Again, all your modern English translations will spell this out and will save you months of traditional Hebrew study. As modern English translations remain pretty accurate in giving the gender, number, and person, I would not concern myself with that either. Next, you will see this, (suff. מלכי). This is simply telling you that this same form can be found with a singular pronominal suffix which again will appear in all English translations, so why bother trying to learn something that someone else who has spent years learning has already given to you. This is followed with: d.6a, which is telling you this is in the declension 6a; for the purposes of this workbook, I won't even attempt to go there.

The only thing that would be of value to you in all this is that last Hebrew word מלך. This is golden; it's your ticket to finding the definition of the word because that is your three-letter root word. So the next thing you will do, is to close your Davidson Analytical Lexicon, reopen it and start again, this time looking up the word melek מלך in the lexicon. You will find that word on page 491 in the middle of the left-hand column beginning in bold Hebrew letters:

מלך ו מלך fut. ימלך – I. *to reign, to be king*, with על

As you continue to read down the section, Davidson will give many different forms of this word and its usages. Sometimes you will find an identical root word used twice with different meanings. Keep in mind that even though the meaning is different, there is a relationship or common root found among all of these definitions. For instance, you will find the root word

לו with the Roman numeral *I.* before it. Then there is the definition of *"to lodge, remain or pass."* Below that you will find the identical root word, only this time it has a Roman numeral *II.* before it. This is followed by the definition of *to complain, murmur.* You must remember that Hebrew is a relationship language and you must continually look for relationships. This will be explained in future chapters, but just pause for a moment and think, what is the relationship between lodging, remaining and complaining and murmuring? One thing that comes to mind is Benjamin Franklin's quote, "Fish and visitors smell in three days." It was when the children of Israel in the wilderness wanderings came to lodge or remain at a certain place that they began to complain. As long as they were moving, they were not apt to murmur or complain.

Conclusion:

I have just introduced you to the two most valuable tools for Hebrew word study. The interlinear, to find a Hebrew word and the Lexicon, to define the word. Both can be found for free online, or you can purchase them in printed copies for less than $50.00. We also offer an online interlinear and lexicon on our website at www.chaimbentorah.com.

These tools are readily available and there for you to use. It does not take years of learning to use them. It will take a little practice getting used to the Hebrew Alphabet and looking up words, but like any discipline, such as learning a new computer program, after a week or two of use, you will be operating like a pro.

QUESTIONS

1. What is a Hebrew lexicon?

2. What is the advantage of the BDB over the Davidson Analytical Lexicon?

3. What is the advantage of the Davidson Analytical Lexicon over the BDB?

4. What is an interlinear?

5. Name one website where you can find both an interlinear and a lexicon.

6. What is a triliteral roots?

7. What do we mean when we say the Hebrew is a relationship language?

8. Why is it important to consider the Semitic origin of a Hebrew word?

9. Modern Israeli Hebrew is the based upon the Classical Hebrew, but it is not the same and may not even be considered a Semitic language. True False

10. Look up Psalms 23:4 in an interlinear and find the Hebrew word for cup and then look it up in a lexicon and tell me something interesting about the word cup.

ANSWERS

1. It is a dictionary of Hebrew words listed in Alphabetical order giving the definition of a Hebrew word.

2. The BDB is more comprehensive than the Davidson Analytical Lexicon showing Hebrew word's relationship to other Semitic languages.

3. You can look up a word in the Davidson Analytical Lexicon as it is found in the Hebrew text. With the BDB you must first determine the three-letter root word to look up a word.

4. An interlinear shows the Hebrew text with the corresponding English words located above or below the Hebrew word.

5. Either Bible Hub or Study Light. When you type in a Scripture reference into a search engine one or the other or both of the websites will be listed on the first page.

6. All Hebrew words are built on a three-letter root word called a triliteral root.

7. Words in Hebrew are related to each other when spelled the same or share a similar root even though they may have entirely different meanings, there is still some relationship between the various definitions.

8. Many Semitic words share a similar origin and that origin could shed light upon the definition of a particular Hebrew word.

9. True

10. Kavas כוס This word also means a pelican. This should prompt you to do some research online about pelicans which in ancient times was considered the same bird as a stork. You may recall the legend of a stork delivering babies. That is because a stork or pelican is noted for its tender care of its young. It was believed that if there was no food to feed a young pelican the mother would feed it on her with blood and there was even a belief that if a chick died the mother would raise it from the dead with her own blood. Hence David may have been thinking of the loving-kindness of God overflowing from a symbol of nurturing and caring.

LESSON 3
MEANINGS BEHIND HEBREW LETTERS

LESSON 3
MEANINGS BEHIND THE HEBREW LETTERS

In my book *Learning God's Love Language: Personal Hebrew Word Study*, I went into detail on the history of the Hebrew alphabet and the development of the Square Script. It is believed by many Jews that the Square Script was developed to maintain the purity of the Hebrew language through its writing system. Throughout the history of the Hebrew people, their leaders would teach of our relationship to God using using certain phonic sounds that were put into the form of symbols or letters. Before the development of the Square Script, the Hebrews borrowed from the Canaanite Script, which was built upon pagan symbols. The Square Script was developed to express symbols that show our relationship to God Jehovah and His to us.

Throughout the ages, the sages and rabbis assigned many different meanings to these letters and then used these meanings as a memorization tool to help explain the original or deeper meaning behind certain Hebrew words. This is not intended to be a linguistical tool but a devotional tool used to help you meditate on God's Word.

During the middle ages, families would play with these meanings almost like modern families playing board games. The children would offer their opinions as to what a Hebrew word would mean based upon its letters as well as the parents contributing their insights. They would seek to come to some conclusion or understanding that would teach a moral lesson or a lesson about their relationship with God and God's to them.

There's no proof that God intended to have a built-in commentary in each Hebrew word, yet the meanings behind the letters, when applied often, help to shed a deeper understanding of of a word through the meditation on that word and passage of Scripture.

After you have looked up a Hebrew word in your lexicon and studied it in light of the definitions given and its Semitic origins, you may wish to move a little further to see if there is more to be discovered about that word. The next step would be to examine the word, letter by letter.

After many years of studying Jewish literature, I have compiled a list of various meanings that, at one time or another was applied to the Hebrew letters. The following is a list of all the meanings I have uncovered from thirty-five years of study. I do not consider it an exhaustive list, but it does give us enough to work with. I have listed the meanings as *Primary*, which are the most common applications. The other applications I have found were, on one or more occasion, applied but not as often as the primary meanings. Then I discovered that each letter had a negative application, or as one writer called it a *Shadow*, which is a term I like to use.

MEANINGS BEHIND THE HEBREW LETTERS

ALEPH	PRIMARY:	God, Unity, Headship
א	OTHER:	Stillness, fire, oneness, mastery, humility, purity, repentance, the line between heaven and earth.
	SHADOW:	Doctrine or theology that is in error, ambivalence toward God.

BETH	PRIMARY: commandments.	Heart, house, shelter
ב	OTHER:	Duality, place of beginning, blessing, creation,
	SHADOW:	Feeling spiritually superior to others

GIMMEL	PRIMARY:	Loving kindness, Culmination, Nourishment
ג	OTHER:	Courage, place of beginning, running after someone or something to perform a good deed.
	SHADOW:	Misguided missionary zeal.

DALETH:	PRIMARY:	Door, Gateway, Portal, Knowledge
ד	OTHER:	Binding with God, Physical world, Path.
	SHADOW:	False humility, Excessive humility

HEI:	PRIMARY:	Breath of God, God's presence, Feminine nature of God.
ה	OTHER:	Mercy, Creative power of God, Revelation
	SHADOW:	Self-deception, Self-pity.

VAV:	PRIMARY:	Connection between heaven and earth. Man, Completion.
ו	OTHER:	Redemption, Transformation, Relationship between two people. Relationship between man and God.
	SHADOW:	Anguish, Addiction, Dependence upon someone or something other than God.

ZAYIN:	PRIMARY:	Involvement with God. God fighting or defending us.
ז	OTHER:	Sustenance, Sabbath.
	SHADOW:	Struggle, Inappropriate aggression, Laziness

CHETH:	PRIMARY:	Joining of man to God, Grace, Life, Bonding with God through a spiritual connection (Christian term would be Salvation through Jesus Christ)
ח	OTHER:	Prophetic dreams, Infinity. Moving forward.
	SHADOW:	Sin, Destruction, Paralyzing fear, Rudeness, Pushiness.

TETH:	PRIMARY:	Good, Inward Examination, Divine Light.
ט	OTHER:	Travel, Repentance, Cultivate the creative feminine power and the potent masculine power.
	SHADOW:	Unrealistic optimism, Lacking depth, Easy answers.

YOD	PRIMARY:	Heavenly message (messenger), Spirituality.
י	OTHER:	Authenticate, Close friendship, Momentum, Creation.
	SHADOW:	No foundation, Irrational act

KAP	PRIMARY:	Cup, Container, Empty or full heart, Palm of the hand.
כ	OTHER:	Possession, Willpower, Intentionality, Empty mind to be filled with God's thoughts.
	SHADOW:	Arrogance, Seeking your own will and not God's.

LAMED:	PRIMARY:	Reaching up to heaven for Divine knowledge, Receiving Divine knowledge into your heart.
ל	OTHER:	Learning, Teaching, Purpose, Prayer
	SHADOW:	Narrow thinking, Self-importance, Workaholic.

MEM:	PRIMARY:	Open knowledge
FINAL MEM:	PRIMARY:	Hidden knowledge
מ ם	OTHER:	Perfection, Completion.
	SHADOW:	Drowning in sorrow, Destructive passion.

NUN:	PRIMARY:	Emergence, Faith, Breaking down walls of separation. Swimming among the ebb and flow of currents.
נ	OTHER:	Prophecy, Revelation of light.
	SHADOW:	Coolness, Aloofness.

SAMEK	PRIMARY:	God's protection. God's support.
ס	OTHER:	Abundance, Memory, Shelter, Joy, Mysteries of God.
	SHADOW:	Too dependent upon a person or thing.

AYIN:	PRIMARY:	Spiritual insight, Discernment
ע	OTHER:	Sight, Spirituality, Inner reflection, Consciousness.
	SHADOW:	Greed, Coveting.

PEI:	PRIMARY:	Speech, Freedom, Silence
פ	OTHER:	Communication, To speak inspiration, Speaking God's Heart, Speaking your heart. Healing.
	SHADOW:	Talking too much, Gossiping.

SADE:	PRIMARY:	Humility, Righteousness.
צ	OTHER:	Submission to the Divine will, Charity, Love
	SHADOW:	Self-righteousness, Letting failure discourage you.

QOP ק	PRIMARY:	Holiness, Sanctification.
	OTHER:	Sacrifice, Receiving, Call of God, Growth
	SHADOW:	Condemning others in a fellowship, Being an un-holy influence.

RESH ר	PRIMARY:	Holy Spirit, Power of God, Repentance.
	OTHER:	Willingness, Bend in a path, Turning point.
	SHADOW:	God's chastisement, Prideful man, Judgmental, Abusing power of leadership.

SHIN, SINE שׁ שׂ	PRIMARY:	Peace, Joy, Divine power, God's passion
	OTHER:	Wholeness, Completion, End's nearness, God's Filling, Consuming passion, Fire.
	SHADOW:	Corruption, Destruction, Consumed by anger, lust or jealousy.

TAW ת	PRIMARY:	Truth, Perfection, Praise
	OTHER:	Prayer from the heart,
	SHADOW:	Clinging to a relationship that is hindering one's relationship with God.

THE MISSING LETTER ?	PRIMARY:	To be at peace with what God will reveal to you.
	SHADOW:	Abandoning the present for the future.

APPLICATION OF THE MEANINGS BEHIND HEBREW LETTERS

Most of us may recall when we were in high school, and we were assigned a locker. We would secure it with a combination lock to ensure that only we, who knew that combination, could open the locker. I am sure that hundreds of other students had used the locker before I did, yet I was guaranteed that only I could enter it, because I had the combination to that lock. The combination consisted of three numbers. I would spin the dial on the front of the lock to the right and stop on the number 27, then I would spin the dial back to 18 and then to the right to 7, and my lock would open. If I was just one digit off, the lock would not open, and I could not get into my locker. No one else had that number and what was in the locker belonged to me and me alone.

I believe God's Word operates on the same principle. Billions of people have access to God's Word. The Bible is like a big locker room, and everyone has their own personal combination lock. No one else has your personal combination and through the Holy Spirit's guidance, you can access meanings behind the three letter root words to discover your own personal message from God, that belongs to you and you alone. It is God being a personal God to you. It is something between you and God, and it is not shared with anyone else.

As you look at the various meanings behind each letter you may wonder, "Just which meaning do I apply to each letter and which combination?." God has a combination for you and you alone that He wants to share.

So why don't we start spinning our combination lock and see if we can unlock our Bible and find some hidden commentary in a Hebrew word? I will walk you through as I reveal my own combination to a word, then I will let you go to your locker to see if you can open it up with your own personal combination.

Let us take a look at Psalms 23:2 "He will cause me to lie down in green pastures: He will lead me beside the still waters." I feel a little surge in my spirit when I read the words *green pas-tures*. I look at this word נאות pastures and I can't help but think, what good is that? I don't eat grass; I would much rather lay in a bed than on the grass. Sorry, I am just not an outdoor type. Some are, and for them, that is a pleasant thought to lie down in green pastures. For me, I just think of bugs and little sticky things in the grass and a hot sun when I would much rather have air conditioning.

So I go to my interlinear and look at this verse. In the interlinear I find two words for green pastures or grass, but my interlinear renders these words as *oasis of vegetation*. This is similar to green grass but again different. This tells me that there is no one perfect or clearly defined rending. The word for *oasis* is bin'avath בנאות. I am not sure if this is the word for *green* or *pastures*, an oasis could be both. I go to my Davidson lexicon and look up the word just as I find it in my interlinear, so I can see its three-letter root word.

If you are new at this, it may take a half hour or longer, but if you do it enough, it will come quicker and easier. It is just like learning a new software program. The first time you use it you are convinced you will never get the hang of it. But after a couple weeks you are doing backflips with the program. So please, hang in there, don't expect to find these words instantly at first. Once you become familiar with it, it will flow very easy.

Ok, here it is in the Davidson lexicon בנאות, and when I look to the right of the line, I see the three letter word נאה. That is my root word. I went through all that effort just for that. But it is worth it, because now I have the key to finding the meaning behind this word בנאות. I open up my Davidson lexicon again and look up נאה. Here I find the meaning behind this word which is *to sit, dwell, to be beautiful, seats, habitation, flocks, herd, and pastures.* Ok, I know that is not the word for *green*. Yet, what does this mean, what do all these words have in common? I meditate on that, let the Holy Spirit speak to me. I find that the one thing they all have in common is it is something pleasant, restful and beautiful. I think my interlinear hit the nail on the head with the word oasis that word fits all these definitions given by my Davidson Lexicon.

Ok, now the word that is rendered as *green* or *vegetation* as shown in my interlinear. This is the word *deshe'* דשא. This time I am going to look the word up in my BDB. Checking the back of my Strong's Concordance, I find the root word just happens to be דשא. Being a Hebrew teacher, I knew that without looking it up, but I want to give you a guide to follow. So I go to my BDB and look this up and I find it means *grass, green, a tender herb, a sprout, which by analogy means grass.* I find that it comes from an Aramaic word meaning *something springing out of the earth.*

So basically what I am getting from my lexicons and Strong's Concordance is that God will lead me to a pleasant habitation on tender grass. In other words green pastures. Yeah, I know, nothing really profound out of that. This is where most people usually quit. But you did not purchase this workbook to go just this far, you want something more, so let me give you more.

Let us move beyond the lexicons and go to our locker and begin to spin the dial on our lock and see if it opens up a hidden treasure for us.

The word that we have for pastures is from the root word *na'ah* נאה. The first letter is a Nun נ. When I think of a pasture or place of a pleasant habitation what particular meaning of the Nun נ would apply to this. Well, take a look at our chart and we find that we have *emergence, faith, breaking down walls of separation, swimming among the ebb and flow of currents, prophecy or revelation of light.* Go ahead, pick any one, two, three or more that you feel would apply to a pleasant habitation that God would bring you to. For me, a place of pleasant habitation would be a place where I am just resting in *faith* with God. Maybe for you it is a place where *walls of separation are broken down,* maybe for someone else it is a *place of emergence* from a difficult situation. Don't pick the one I pick just because I picked it. Pick the one that fits your situation. Colossians 3:15 says to let the peace of God rule your heart. The word rule in Greek means to umpire. Let the peace of God be your umpire. Pick the meaning that you feel the most peace about.

The next letter is the Aleph א. Now I have picked for the Nun נ the word *faith*. So I am asking myself, just how finding a place of pleasant rest relates to faith? The Aleph represents *stillness, fire, oneness mastery, humility, purity, repentance, the line between heaven and earth, faith in unity with God.* I think I find two meanings here which would fit my personal journey with God, and that is unity with God. This place of rest comes with *faith (Nun נ) in my unity with God (Aleph א).*

Finally, we come to the last letter which is the Hei ה. I am finding this pleasant place of rest in my faith in the unity I have with God because of the Hei ה. What does the Hei ה provide? We have *mercy, creative power of God, revelation, Breath of God, God's presences and the feminine nature of God.* Actually, they all fit, and no problem if I put them all in there. But for me personally, at this point in my life that sense of peace, that pleasant resting place with God that I find in my unity with Him comes from the Hei representing His presence.

But this is more than just a pasture, it is a green pasture. So what about this greenness? Is there anything that speaks to me there? Well, this is the word *deshe'* דֶּשֶׁא. I am at rest in the pasture because it is *green*. That first letter is the Daleth ד. The Daleth ד is a *doorway, gateway* or *portal to knowledge.* It is also a *binding with God and the physical world or a pathway.* I am personally moving my combination lock to the word *portal.* For me this place of *rest in unity with God in His presence is a portal.* A *portal* to what? It is a *portal* to the next letter which is the Shin שׁ. The Shin שׁ speaks to us of *wholeness, completion, end's nearness, God's filling, God's consuming passion, fire, peace, joy, divine power, God's passion.*

For me personally, this one is a no-brainer. This place of *peace, rest, in a unity with God feeling His presence is a portal to His consuming passion.*

That brings us to the last letter which is again the Aleph א. This time I am choosing the meaning of *a line between heaven and earth.*

So, from the lexicons, we learn that *green pastures* are a place of *pleasant habitation of green grass.* From studying these words letter by letter, I find God's built-in commentary telling me that *green pastures* are a place where my *faith* נ *brings me into unity with God* א *bringing me into his presence* ה. *The green grass is a portal* ד *to the consuming passion of God* שׁ *which gives me a connection between heaven and earth* א.

Conclusion

In the Middle Ages, Jewish families would apply these meanings to Hebrew words as sort of a family activity or fun time together. The children and adults would all suggest the application of meanings to letters and discuss their value and worth to the Scripture passage. This was a form of entertainment like a board game is today only you did not have the competition and the element of winner or losers only everyone offering their personal insight and drawing a conclusion.

Try this in a Bible study. Gather two or three other believers who are interested in searching for a deeper understanding of Scripture and take a little time to play around with the different combinations. You will be amazed at how quickly time passes and that fact that you have spent one to two hours in the word without realizing it.

I have led Bible studies with pastors discussing the possible application of various meanings of the Hebrew letters. We agreed to only spend one-half hour discussing because we were all so busy. Yet after two hours, our discussions were still going strong. Studying the Word of God suddenly became exciting. Not only that, I would hold these discussions with pastors from many different doctrinal positions and yet there was never any discussion of doctrine or theology because we were studying the Word of God and its personal application, not theology. We were venturing down new avenues that their books and church denominations never bother to walk down. We were united under only one flag and that was our love for God and His Word.

EXERCISE

Psalms 23:4, "Yea, when I am walking through the valley of the shadow of death, I will be awed by no evil, for You are with me. Your rod and Your staff, they will *comfort* me."

The word for *comfort* is nacham נחם *to comfort, feel pity, grieve, repent, mourn and feel compassion.* It is rooted in an old Persian word for giving a sigh. What do all these words have in common? Write out one to two words, or a sentence which could encompass all these other words.

Your rod and your staff _____me.

Write out a word for word definition of nacham נחם – comfort.

Nun נ

_____

_____

_____

_____

_____

Cheth ח

_____

_____

_____

_____

_____

Final Mem ם

_____

_____

_____

_____

_____

Write out your commentary of nacham נחם comfort from you letter by letter analysis.

_____

_____

_____

_____

_____

POSSIBLE ANSWER

Thy rod and thy staff *cause me grief that leads to my repentance.*

LESSON 4

GEMATRIA

LESSON 4
GEMATRIA

Revelation 13:18, "Here is the wisdom. The one who has understanding must count the number of the beast, for it is a number of mankind, and its number is six hundred sixty-six."

Anyone who is interested in prophecy and teachings about the antichrist has at one time, or another contemplated the number 666. They look for it on their credit cards, in names, dates, places, computer programs or anywhere else that might give them a clue as to the identity of the antichrist. What they are doing is working with an old Jewish practice of Scriptural study called the Gematria. The Gematria is taking the numerical value of a Hebrew word and finding another Hebrew word with the same numerical value and substituting that word in a verse of Scripture to discover some deeper meaning in that passage. Such a practice takes wisdom in knowing when and when not to use the numerical association, and there have been many books published that demonstrate a lack of wisdom in making that association with 666. It also takes an understanding of the Gematria to make the proper application, and again, there has been an equal number of books that demonstrate this lack of understanding concerning 666.

This lesson is meant to provide some of that understanding. As far as the necessary wisdom goes, I cannot give you that, only the Holy Spirit can give you the wisdom. So let's focus on what we can accomplish, and that is an understanding of what the Gematria is and what it is not, and how it is used.

What the Gematria is not, is numerology. It is not a method of fortune telling or giving you good luck. I was on the elevator in a high-rise building and discovered that it did not have a thirteenth floor. I asked a maintenance engineer in the building about it, and he said the building was built with the intention of hosting a global community. He said many visitors from foreign nations, even prominent well-educated visitors find the number thirteen to be a symbol of evil or bad luck, and if a business were located on a thirteenth floor, it could affect business relationships with those visitors. The Gematria has nothing to do with one's fortune or misfortune.

It has nothing to do with foretelling future events, although I have read where the Gematria was used to discover a future event. Talmudists are obsessed with the number 6. Even the

Holocaust Memorial in Washington D.C. was designed using multiples of 6. Man was created on the sixth day which is why six is considered the number of man in Judaism. The Star of David has six points, three pointing up three pointing down.

Leviticus 25:13, "In the year of this jubilee *you will return*

each man to his possession." In this passage the word for *you will return* is *tasheuvu* תֹּשֻׁבוּ. However, as it is written in the Hebrew Bible it is grammatically incorrect, the word should be spelled תֹּשׁוּבוּ. For centuries Talmudists have argued as to why the Vav ו was omitted in the Hebrew text when it should, grammatically, be there. They went to the Gematria to see if they could find an answer. They added up the numerical value of the word *tasheuvu, you will return* תֹּשׁוּבוּ but included the missing Vav and got the number 708. When Talmudists write a year they ignore the millennia for reasons I do not understand. So they added the millennia of 5000 and got 5708. They declared that the Jews would return to their homeland in 5708 on the Jewish calendar. Then to explain the missing Vav ו which is the number 6 they determined this represented 6,000,000 and declared that before the Jews could return to the land of Israel 6,000,000 Jews must vanish. Of course, this was just the rambling musings of Talmudists during the nineteenth century and nobody paid much attention until the year 5708 came along. For you see 5708 on the Jewish calendar happens to be 1948 on the Julian Calendar, the year that Israel became a nation. But what about that missing Vav? Why was the Vav missing in Leviticus 25:13? Did 6,000,000 Jews vanish before the return of the Jews to Israel? The approximate number of the Jews who perished during the Holocaust was 6,000,000.

As you can see the Talmudic Jews have turned the study of the Gematria into a complex science. I do not understand how they arrived at the Vav representing 6,000,000 Jews vanishing before the return of the Jews to Israel or why they used the fifth millennia to put before the 708, but it either worked or it was an amazing coincidence.

As you work with the Gematria you will discover some amazing coincidences or maybe it is just a God incident, only you can decide, but as you work with the Gematria, you will discover some amazing things.

On the next page is a chart of the numerical value of each Hebrew letter. This may serve as a guide as you seek to develop the numerical value of Hebrew words.

Numerical Value of Hebrew Letters

1	א
2	ב
3	ג
4	ד
5	ה
6	ו
7	ז
8	ח
9	ט
10	י
20	ך כ
30	ל
40	ם מ
50	ן נ
60	ס
70	ע
80	ף פ
90	ץ צ
100	ק
200	ר
300	שׁשׂ
400	ת

Now let's see how we can apply some fundamental principles of the Gematria to our own personal study. We can take the word for *I weep* which in the Hebrew is the word beki בכי. Now looking at our numerical chart we need to determine the numerical value of this word. It is spelled Beth ב = 2, Kap כ = 20 and Yod י = 10 for a total numerical value of 32. Now we need to find a Hebrew word that also has a value of 32. The word for heart is lev לב. This is spelled with a Lamed ל = 30 and Beth ב = 2. The word for heart and the word for I weep both have a value of 32. According to the ancient sages when two words have an identical numerical value, there is a relationship between these words. What is the relationship between the heart and weeping? Weeping comes from the heart. Sometimes when you pray or worship God you will begin to weep. That is an indication that you are praying or worshipping God with your heart. If you watch a movie and begin to cry you know that movie has touched your heart.

You can do this with phrases as well. For instance, Genesis 1:28 commands that we are to be *fruitful and multiply*. This is directly speaking of the intimacy between a man and woman. In Hebrew, this phrase is *peru* פרו *u* ו *rebu* רבו. Add all these letters up with a numerical value of 500. You have Pei פ = 80, Resh ר = 200, Vav ו = 6, Vav ו = 6, Resh ר = 200, Beth ב = 2 and Vav ו = 6 which totals 500. So what word or words do 500 equal that shows a relationship? The Jews were instructed to light two candles to usher in the Sabbath. Candle is the word *ner* נר. The Nun נ has a value of 50 and the Resh ר has a value of 200. Candle נר has the value of 250. However, the instruction is to light two candles. 250 + 250 equals 500. The Jews believe that the intimacy between a man and woman was not sinful for the Jewish law decrees: "Let the holy act be performed on the holy night." It is a Jewish custom during a wedding for the father and mother of the bride and bridegroom to walk down the aisle each with a candle showing the holiness of the marriage. Two candles grace the Sabbath table to show the holiness of the intimacy between a man and woman and that it is also a mitzvah (good deed) of the holy day. The husband and wife are intimate with each other to complete their worship of God, but it is not to be between them alone but to share an intimacy with God as well. In fact, the intimate nature of the Sabbath is to reflect our intimate, love relationship with God. All that from the Gematria.

Numbers have always carried some biblical significance. Below are just some of the symbolic meanings behind numbers that may be found in the Bible.

1	Unity
2	Union, Joining together
3	God Head
4	Creation
5	Grace, Mercy, Semi Completion
6	Man, Satan, Imperfection

7.   Completion, Always Means God

8   New Beginnings, New Birth, Salvation

9   Divine Completeness

10   Absolute Completion

11   Chaos, Judgment

12   Earthly Governments

13   Rebellion, Sin

14   Deliverance

15   Rest

16   Love, Affection, Passion

17   Victory Bondage

18   Captivity

19   Faith

20   Redemption

50   Holy Spirit

70   Israel and fulfillment

100   Election, Fulfillment

1000   Glory of God

You may wonder if there is a book that gives the numerical values of all the Hebrew words, to save you the time of calculating each word. I have never found such a book but I have found a website which does provide this information. It is found on a site called Bible Wheel (Although the author has discredited his own theories on the Bible Wheel his section on the Gematria was produced through a computer program and the numerical values are accurate.) We have provided a link to this site on our website. If you go to www.chaimbentorah.com on the home page menu you will see link for Gematria. Click on that and it will take you to the page on Bible Wheel's website where you will see a little box with the word Gematria next to it. Type in the numerical value of the word you are interested in. This will send you to a page which will list all the other words in the Hebrew Bible that have the same numerical value. Look down the list and see if there are any words which might have a relationship to the word you are studying in the Bible. If there is check it out with the context of that verse and see if it can provide any deeper insight.

Conclusion:

Again this is a little tool to use when you are seeking a deeper understanding of a particular Hebrew word. If you play the little parlor or family game I mentioned in the last chapter using the meanings behind Hebrew words you can also play around with the word's numerical value as well and compare those words with other words sharing the same numerical value.

Thanks to the internet and modern technology you do not have to spend days, weeks even months trying to locate another word with the same value, just a click of your mouse will

accomplish what took rabbis in the last century months to achieve.

EXERCISES

1. What is the numerical value of the name of God YHWH יהוה?

י‎_____

ה‎_____

ו‎_____

ה‎_____

Total _____

2. What is the numerical value of the word for one echad אחד?

א‎_____

ח‎_____

ד‎_____

Total_____ X 2 _____

Can you find a relationship between these final numbers of John 10:30 "I and [my] Father are one."

_____

_____

_____

_____

3. The Aleph א which are two YODs and a Vav יוי what is the numerical value of these letters.

י _____

ו _____

י _____

Total _____

What does that this tell you about the Aleph א?

4. What is the numerical value for the word love ahavah אהבה?

א _____

ה _____

ב _____

ה _____

Total_____X2_____

What does the value of love multiplied by 2 tells of the love between two people?

5. What is the numerical value of word for woman ishah השה?

ה _____

שׁ _____

ה _____

Total_____

What is the numerical value of word for honey dabash דבשׁ?

ד _____

ב _____

שׁ _____

Total_____

How is this significant if a husband calls his wife *honey*?

ANSWERS

1. 26

2. 13X2=26 Jesus is one echad = 13 and the father is one echad = 13 the two together equal 26 for one YHWH

3. 26 The Aleph is the letter for Jehovah God

4. 13 13+13 = 26 God resides in the love between two people.

5. Woman = 306, Honey = 306. A man's wife is as sweet as honey.

LESSON 5

HEBREW WORD
PLAYS

LESSON 5
HEBREW WORD PLAYS

What Is A Word Play?

Wordplays in the Hebrew Bible are an accepted linguistical phenomenon among Bible scholars, although many tend to overlook them as they can be very complex and there is a tendency to read more into a passage than was intended by the writers. However, wordplays do exist and are often referenced by many notable scholars and commentators. Yet, we are dealing with the inspired word of God not just a piece of ancient literature. If there are wordplays, God had intent behind the wordplay and it, therefore, becomes more than a literary exercise. It can become a study for Christians, depending on the Holy Spirit to discern if an apparent wordplay does exist and if it does, just what is the message behind the wordplay.

Word plays are common in all languages. We have many such wordplays in English. They are often used as literary devices to further explain a matter, make a poetic statement or more often, to just add humor. Puns are the greatest example of such wordplays. For instance: "Two loaves of bread wanted to get married, so they eloafed." This is a play on the word elope.

"I decided not to go to Pisa, but I was leaning towards it." This is a play on the word lean as it is commonly used with the Leaning Tower of Pisa.

"I yam always very happy to eat sweet potatoes." This is a play on the secondary word for sweet potatoes, *yam* which sounds like *am*.

"New light bulb invented? Enlighten me." This is a play on two words that are similar *enlighten* and *light*.

Ultimately, many word plays are simply just puns. However, let's take a look at how a word-*play* will *play* out in Hebrew.

Confusing the Context

One example of a wordplay is to confuse the context where a word is used. For instance, there is an essential oil named *Joy* because its fragrance creates a euphoric feeling. Hence one may make a play on the word *joy* by confusing the context. You could say, "Old Chinese proverb says, 'He who puts oil on top shelf, jump for *joy*.'" The word *litter* has a meaning of throwing trash on the ground. The word *fine* means paying a penalty or something that is good and appropriate. Hence you can make a play on the context of these words by saying, "I saw a sign, 'Fine for Littering' so I thought it was a good place to throw my trash." *Litter* is a reference to a substance used to absorb cat waste so you may ask, "If I throw a cat out the car window, is that cat *litter*?"

Words that Sound Alike

There are puns where words sound alike, for instance, if one asks what a Hoosier is, you could reply, "An upright vacuum cleaner." You are speaking of a product known as a Hoover which sounds similar to Hoosier.

Alliteration

Hebrew has some different types of wordplays. For instance, there is the alliterative type. Alliteration is the repetition of the same sounds or the same kinds of sounds at the beginning of words or in stressed syllables of an English language phrase such as Peter Piper Picked a Peck of Pickled Peppers. However, this only plays out when read in Hebrew and not English.

For instance, in Song of Solomon 4:4 we have, "Your neck is like the tower of David built for an armory, on which a thousand shields hang, all shields of mighty men." You have the word talpiyyot לתלפיות which is rendered as *armory*. This produces the alliteration (repetition of the same sounding words) with the words for *thousands* אלפ *'elep* and *hang* תלוי *taluy*.

Parallelism

There is also a type of wordplay in Hebrew called parallelism. This is where a single word bears two different meanings where one meaning parallels what precedes, and the other meaning what follows. For instance in Song of Solomon 2:12 you have. "The flowers appear on the earth: the time of the singing has come and the voice of the turtle-dove is heard in our land." The word *singing* is *zamar* זמר which also means *pruning*. The first meaning of *singing* refers to the turtledoves and the *pruning* goes back to the flowers.

Bilingual Word Plays

Something not often considered is that Biblical writers often engage in bilingual wordplay. For instance, Isaiah 10:8, "For he says, Are not my princes altogether kings?" The word used for princes *sar* שׂרי is a pun on the Akkadian word *sarru* which is the word for king. This will, of course, be difficult to spot if you are not familiar with other Semitic languages, although your BDB will show you some of these words.

For the most part, these word plays are just interesting poetic devices and add no real depth to our understanding of a passage. As with all literature, we can enter into a classroom debate over the meaning behind the wordplay or if a wordplay exists to begin with. However, keep in mind that are dealing with the God's Word, the inspired Word of God, so you could assume that there must be intent behind these wordplays other than a mere literary device.

Esoteric Word Play

In Hebrew, we also have a form of wordplay that employs the esoteric (private, secret or confidential) nature of the Hebrew language and alphabet. For instance, we see in the story of Esther that her Hebrew name was *Hadassah* הדסה but her Persian name was *Esther* אסתר. Esther was a derivative of the name of the Near Eastern goddess Ishtar and is a Persian word *satar* meaning *star*. Hadassah comes from the root word *hadas* הדס which means *myrtle*. The myrtle plant is shaped like a star. So we do see a little bilingual wordplay on Esther's name. Can there be an even deeper play on the name Esther and Hadassah? It is possible that God is telling the entire story of Esther in her name. The name Esther אסתר is spelled Aleph – God, Samek – to be hidden, Taw – truth, and Resh – turning away. In other words, *God* hid the *truth* of Esther's Jewish heritage so He could use her to *turn away* the wrath of Hamon.

The Hebrew people knew their Queen was really Hadassah הדסה which is spelled Hei – the presence of God, Daleth – a doorway, and Samek – protection, shelter, support. Embodied in Hadassah was the *presence* of God and He would use her as a *doorway* to His *protection, shelter and support.*

If you even wondered why there were so many begats in the Bible you might explore the meaning behind the names in these begats. The meanings behind the names and letters may tell a story.

Shared Letters, Shared Meanings

Another interesting play on words used by esoteric rabbis is showing how shared letters suggest a shared meaning. For instance, the word *kever* קבר means *grave*. Esoteric rabbis look at this word and see that if they rearrange the letters to form בקר *boker* they have the word for *morning*. The very word for grave *kever* קבר is telling us that our final resting place is but the *morning* of our new existence with Jesus in heaven.

Let's take a word from Scripture in Isaiah 61:3, "... to appoint to those who mourn in Zion, to give to them beauty instead of ashes..." A former student pointed out that God simply took the word for *ashes 'eper* אֵפֶר and rearranged the letters to *pe'er* פְּאֵר which is the word for *beauty.* Using the same letters only rearranging this God turns our beauty to ashes. You will find rabbis throughout Jewish literature doing this same thing with Hebrew words to enhance their understanding of God's Word. But we are not finished yet. Let's rearrange these letters once more to *rapha'* רְפָא and that gives us the Hebrew word for *healing.* God will not only rearrange the letters to give us beauty for ashes, but he will also continue to rearrange the letters to heal us of all the wounds associated with these ashes.

We can still go further if we look at how all this is going to take place. We have three letters which teach us of ashes, beauty, and healing. How does God heal us from the ashes and turn it into something beautiful? He does it with the Aleph א, his power; through the Pei פ our speaking words of the Resh ר which is repentance. With mouth confession is made unto salvation.

Acronyms

Yes, the Biblical Hebrew does have acronyms according to the Talmud. This may not be considered a wordplay, but I am putting it under this heading as an opportunity to point out its existence. In the Babylonian Talmud Sotar 10a-b we find the sages explaining the reason Abraham planted tamarisk trees to worship God in Genesis 21:33. Biblical scholars have debated for centuries as to the reason Scripture mentions Abraham planting tamarisk trees in the same breath as worshipping God. Certain sages see the Hebrew word for tamarisk אֵשֶׁל as an acronym. The word is spelled Aleph א which is the first letter in the word *'akila* אָכַל which means *food.* The next letter is a Shin שׁ which is the first letter for the word *setiya* שְׁתָה which means *drink* and Lamed ל which is the first letter for *levan* לוּן which means *to lodge.* The sages concluded that Abraham went into the bed and breakfast business and planted the tamarisk trees as fence around his inn. Seeing the fence the Semitic traveler would recognize the dwelling surrounded by these tamarisks אֵשֶׁל as a place to find, food א drink שׁ and lodging ל. But this hostel really served as more like a coffee house with a religious theme.

The verse further explains that he called upon Jehovah from there. The words *he called* in Hebrew is *vayakrie* which is really in a Hiphal imperfect third person form and should be rendered, *he caused others to call (upon the name Jehovah).* In other words, Abraham caused God's name to be spoken in the mouths of all his guests. The Talmud says, roughly translated: "After they ate and drank they blessed him (Abraham) and Abraham said: 'Have you eaten my food? No, your food and drink were provided by Jehovah, thank and bless Him who spoke the world into being."

There is also another play on the word *'eshal* אֵשֶׁל or tamarisk and that it was not only that he planted these trees, but he used them as a billboard or sign for Semitic travelers would associate the tamarisk as a sort of logo for the hostel business from this acronym.

Conclusion

Word plays are difficult to find. Some people just have a knack for picking out word plays like they have a knack for doing puzzles and crosswords. Some are better at it than others. My study partner seems to have a greater ability at picking out word plays than I do, so I usually consult with her about a seeming wordplay I may discover. Wordplays should not necessarily be done alone, they can add interesting discussion to your parlor game or Bible study mentioned in earlier chapters. If you should find a possible wordplay in the Bible you will have an interesting topic to discuss with Christian friends. It seems children have an uncanny knack for picking up on word plays and enjoy doing it. In fact, you may just learn something from your own children. Jews in the Middle Ages would employ such a game in their family entertainment along with the Gematria and meaning behind letters.

QUESTIONS

1. What are the eight different types of word plays?

   a. _____

   b. _____

   c. _____

   d. _____

   e. _____

   f. _____

   g. _____

   h. _____

2. What is a shared letter, shared meaning word play. Give an example

3. What is a bilingual word play, give an example

4. What is a the difference between a word play in literature and a word play in the Bible?

5. Acronyms can be found in the Bible. True? False?

ANSWERS

1. Types of Wordplays

   • Confusing the context

   • Words that sound alike

   • Alliteration

   • Parallelism

   • Bilingual word plays

   • Esoteric word plays

   • Shared letters, shared meanings

   • Acronyms

2. The word *kever* קבר means *grave*. If they you rearrange the letters to form בקר *boker* they have the word for morning. This tells us that our final resting place is but the *morning* of our new existence with Jesus in heaven.

3. A word from one language making a pun on a similar word from another language. *Sar* שרי is the Hebrew word for prince and is a pun on the Akkadian word *sarru* which is the word for king.

4. In literature, a wordplay is a literary device to further explain a matter, make a poetic statement or more often to just add humor. The Bible, being the inspired and revelatory Word of God would go further as God would be using a wordplay to express a broader and deeper message.

5. True

LESSON 6

LEARNING BY EXAMPLE

Lesson 6
Learning by Example

Some Important Rules Before you Begin

I have given you the background, the tools and where to find the resources to do a Hebrew word study. Now the question remains as to how to implement all this into a word study. I believe the best way is to give you examples of word studies and show how the application is made.

Hebrew word studies must be done within the context of specific passages of Scripture, unlike the New Testament and Greek. Greek is a much more developed language and the New Testament was written over a period of one hundred years. You can take a Greek word in Matthew and see how it is used in Revelation to gain a deeper understanding of that word. A simple dictionary definition is often your best source for doing such a word study.

Where Greek is a much more definitive language, Hebrew tends to be more contextual. Not to say that the context is not important in the New Testament Greek, but that in the Old Testament it is much more important to consider a word in its context. Hebrew is an ambiguous language, and one word could have a wide range of meanings.

The Old Testament was written over a period of 1,500 years. Some words tend to take on new or different meanings over those years. Consider the word *gay* in English. Fifty years ago if I were to say that someone was *gay*, people would think of the person as a happy-go-lucky type. Today one would associate gay with a person's sexual orientation. So we must be careful if we say that a word used in Genesis should be rendered the same way in Malachi. That word has been floating around for over 1,000 years and may have picked up a lot of baggage over that time.

Let me use, for example, the Hebrew word *ra'ah* רעה which is rendered as *evil* in many passages of Scripture but in Psalms 23:1 it is rendered as *shepherd.* You will certainly not want to translate Psalms 23:1 as *the Lord is my evil leader.* The context will pretty well dictate which English word you will plug in there.

However, unlike English, when a word has a similar spelling and different meanings, you need to find the root concept behind the word. For instance, if I am passing through customs and I tell the customs agent that I have a trunk what is he going to think? Is he going to look for a tree log or an elephant's nose? Both words sound and are spelled the same, yet mean entirely different things. The agent will automatically consider the word in its context which would be a reference to a large piece of luggage. In English we would not try to understand the relationship between a tree log, an elephant's nose or a piece of luggage, we just know it is one word with different meanings. However, in the Hebrew, you will need to drill down into that word and find common ground between a tree log, an elephant's nose and a piece of luggage. After some deliberation, you may conclude that all three might be cylinder shaped and therefore the word trunk is rooted in the idea of something shaped like a cylinder. Of course, we do not do that in English, but Hebrew has been a dead language for over 2,500 years. We need to drill down to the very heart and soul of a word to try and understand what a person living 2,500 years ago, speaking Hebrew might have thought and pictured in his mind when he heard certain words.

Say he heard the word *ra'ah* רעה, would he hear *evil* or *shepherd*? The context will tell you but you need to ask, is that all that he hears? This word for evil *ra'ah* רעה is an *evil of consuming passion*. When we hear the word evil we automatically hear something that is bad. But that is not the case to the Semitic ear 2,500 years ago; he hears a consuming passion which may be bad but not necessarily. If one has a consuming passion for drugs, sex, or money, that can be bad. If one has a consuming passion for their child, their mate or for God, that may be a good thing. Thus, that Semitic ear may hear *The Lord is my shepherd* but he is hearing something that we in our modern, Western culture may not hear and that is, *The Lord is my consuming passion, I don't want anything else.*

Final Guidelines for a Hebrew Word Study

Let me give you seven important guidelines to follow when doing a Hebrew word study.

1. Always do a word study within the context of a specific passage of Scripture.

2. The Talmud teaches to never lose sight of the literal meaning of a passage, only seek to go deeper into that passage.

3. Use the internet and any resource that you can find. Use commentaries, lexicons, Strong's Concordance, and Jewish teaching to guide and lead you to think out of the box.

4. Seek God and search for God with all your heart.

5. Love the Lord God with all your soul, heart and mind. If you love Him enough, He will reveal His secrets.

6. Let the peace of God rule your heart. Let the Holy Spirit be your ultimate teacher.

7. Always look for a personal message from God, let Him speak to you.

Devotional Style of Word Study

As I said, you must do a word study within the context of a specific passage of Scripture. I do my word studies in a devotional format. You do not have to do this. However, the key word is devotional. This is not an academic study or even a study to teach a class or preach a sermon, this is a study to gain personal insight or a personal application. The following are studies I have done as simply a journal of my private devotions with God. I offer this only as a guide so you can understand how to make a practical application to what you have learned.

Study #1

Difficult Path - linethiboth לתלפיות

Jeremiah 6:16: "Thus says the LORD*, Stand in the roads! See! Ask for the old paths, Where is the good Way? Then walk there and you will find rest for your inner beings. But they said, We will not walk there."

The word *way* or *path* used in Jeremiah 6:16 is *derekim* דרכם which is in a plural form preceded by the word *al* which is in a construct form. The plural would indicate the word is more appropriately rendered as a *crossroad*. With *al* as a construct to *derekim* would create a picture of one standing at a crossroad trying to decide which road to take.

God is instructing us to first *stand*. There are a number of words in the Hebrew which are translated as *stand*. You have *yatsab* יצב which is a standing to be seen, there is *chamar* חמר which is standing in fear, *quwam* קום which is rising up to stand, *'aman* אמן which is standing firm, immovable, and in this verse you have *'amad* אמד which is standing or pausing to contemplate.

So what are you contemplating when you face a crossroad? The word *'amad* אמד is spelled Aleph א – God, Mem מ – revealed knowledge of God, which opens a Daleth ד – a doorway to God's presence. Hence you are contemplating the revealed knowledge of God that will lead you through a doorway to His presence.

The next thing you are told to do is to *see*. This word is *ra'ah* ראה and is a spiritual seeing as in discernment or as the seeing of a prophet or seer. In this context, it would appear that one is to try to imagine what lies at the end of that road or looking at the consequences of taking that road.

Then we are to ask for the *old way*. The word for *way* or *path* here is *linethiboth* לנתבת and not *derek* דרך. This word comes from the root word, *nathav* נתב which is a path of uncertainty. The word is spelled Nun which shows a path that you follow in faith, Taw that indicates this path is following divine guidance and Beth teaching us that this path will lead us to God's heart.

The word that is rendered *old or ancient* really caught my attention. For the word *old* is *'olam* עלם which has a root meaning of *conceal, hidden, or secret*. We get the idea of old from the fact that the past, like the future, is hidden from us. We can only be certain of the present. Hence, the word is also used for eternity. However, in this context, I read that we are told to ask for the path that is uncertain and hidden. The syntax would suggest that we are to also ask for the *good* path. The word *good* or *tov* טוב means a *path that is in harmony with God*.

Ultimately, this is a path you have to walk in complete faith. This walk will lead to *rest*. The word for *rest* is *raka* רכא which is a *rest that comes suddenly upon you* after going through a turbulent time. It is a play on the word *marag* מרג which means *a threshing machine*. It is a rest that comes after God has taken you through the fires. It is the rest that a prizefighter feels when the bell rings and he goes to his corner. He is still in the fight, but he has a moment (which is another way the word *raka* is used) to catch his breath, receive instruction and encouragement, take a sip of water and regain his strength. It is a picture of flying through a hurricane and coming out into the eye of the hurricane. I read in the National Geographic about the scientists who fly into a hurricane. They said the worst turbulence comes just before they break through to the eye of the hurricane, then everything becomes peaceful. That is *raka* רכא. But like the prizefighter who still has to get back into the ring and the plane must fly back into the hurricane to get home, God will give us rest on our journey to His presence, but we must also get up and continue that journey.

But first, we must *'amad* אמד or pause to prayerfully contemplate our journey to make sure we take the right path, the path that is in harmony with God. We must *'amad* אמד or pause to contemplate our path because we will instinctively choose the path of least resistance and not the path that is *linethiboth* לנתבת *(hidden or uncertain)*. God's perfect will might be the *linethiboth* לנתבת or the more difficult, hidden or uncertain path. When we do *'amad* אמד then we face a decision like Israel, do we take the *linethiboth* לבתבת, the difficult path or the easy path

My personal application is that when I worship God in the general ballroom of His heart, so to speak, we are all celebrating, cheering, dancing and praising. But then I *'amad* אמד or stand or pause to contemplate a small door hidden off in a corner. I *'amad* אמד or consider whether to enter this room for I know what is behind that door. It is a special room, a room apart from all that joy; it is a room where Jesus separates Himself from the celebration and joy in the large ballroom. It is the room He goes into to weep over those who are in pain and suffering and not able to join in the celebration in His ballroom. Do I dare leave this room of joy and praise to enter this hidden chamber to weep with my Savior for those who cannot attend the celebration? Do I dare share in His suffering (Romans 8:17)? Am I willing to leave this hall of joy to take on the pain that my Savior feels and intercede for those He loves and longs to bring into the joy of His salvation? Am I going to be like Israel in Jeremiah 6:16 and say, "I will not walk there." However, if I do choose to walk into this room and weep with

Him, He will share *words (devar)* דבר with me that I can share with those He is weeping for and this knowledge brings me *raka (rest)* רכא.

Analysis

In this study, as with all my studies, I start with some background. For instance, I learned the plural form of the word indicating a crossroad through reading a commentary. Even an Old Testament professor still needs to refer to commentaries for background information. My next step is to look up the words of interest in the interlinear. Once I have the Hebrew word I then move to my lexicon for the various definitions of a particular word. I try to read all the definitions and find a common root that would fit the context of the word in that verse. You will notice I only used the letter meanings on one word. I felt *'amad* was a key word in this verse and I wanted to examine it a little deeper. The other words fit the context nicely and I did not feel any particular need to examine them at any greater depth. Someone else reading this verse might want to examine other words closer. Keep in mind these word studies are a personal study where you are sensitive to the leading, guiding and instruction of the Holy Spirit to give you a personal message from God's Word.

In this next study I also started off with looking the verse up in various commentaries I found online on Bible Hub or Studylight. With that background, I was able to pinpoint the particular words that I wanted to study. With one word, *fire*, I found it beneficial to use the Gematria, and with the word *divide*, I found the letter meanings added a deeper insight. For the word *flame*, I used to the BDB to trace that word to its Semitic root to discover it originated from the sun reflecting off a sword. Note, too, despite all this I continue to pay attention to the literal meaning and I am careful not to leave that behind.

The point is that you do not need to use every tool for every word, only where you feel a need. Relax as you study, use the tools like an artist uses a paintbrush and colors. For one particular scene, he will choose a particular brush and a particular color. Your interlinear, Lexicon, Tracing a Semitic Root, Strong's Concordance, Commentaries, Letter Meanings, Gematria and Wordplays are all tools to create a picture or a work of art for you personally from the Word of God. Some tools you will use often, some you will rarely use, but know how to use them so when the need arises you are ready to put them to us.

Study #2

Psalm 29:7: "The voice of the LORD divides the flames of fire."

There are many interpretations of this Psalm. One is that it is referring to God making a covenant with man. Some commentators say David is referring to the three Hebrew children in the fiery furnace (although David lived long before this event). The most common interpretation is that David wrote this Psalm before a thunderstorm. The fires of flame would represent the lightning, and the voice of God is the thunder.

I suppose it is possible that it was a thunderstorm that prompted this psalm, but one is still left wondering just what David was implying about the nature of God and his relationship with man in this verse. In ancient times, lightning and thunder were said to be the gods battling against each other. Lightning and thunder are an awesome event and does remind one of how powerful God really is.

A demonstration of God's power may be the literal meaning, but David may have seen a little more than this. David was the king of one of the most powerful nations in the world. Maybe he saw himself as the flames of fire being *divided chesev* חצב by the voice of God. David flashes his lightning and God responds with his thunder, which cuts him down to size. The word *divide* חצב is spelled with a Chet - joining with God, Sade – humility and Beth – the heart, suggesting that God's voice draws him away from his own splendor, and humbles him before God.

The word for *fire 'esh* אֵשׁ has a numerical value of 301. The Aleph = 1 and the Shin = 300 for 301. The word for *from or out of fear* or *from or out of distress* is מִירְאִים. The Mem = 40, the Yod = 10, the Resh = 200, the Aleph = 1, the Yod = 10 and the Mem = 40 which also has numerical value of 301. *From* fire can come *fear and distress*. The *blazing or flame* comes from the word *lehev* לַהַב which in its Semitic origins is the glittering of the sun off a sword.

The flames of fire could be a picture of those fears and distress that constantly wear us down. As a king, David lived with constant fear and distress. Perhaps as he sat watching the thunderstorm he saw the lightning flash and it caused him to think about how he could be so at peace one moment and then like a lightning flash he is reminded of some serious problem or situation that he had to confront. Then suddenly right after that flash of lightning, there was thunder, almost like the voice of God cutting or destroying that fearful or distressful situation.

The voice of God is interesting. True there are occasions when the voice of God boomed out and people thought it was thunder. An example is at the baptism of Jesus or the mount of transfiguration. But we also find that the voice of God can be a still small voice. The word *voice* is *qol* קוֹל which means *a noise, a sound, or a report*. The word for voice is spelled with a Qop, Vav, and Lamed and would represent unification between God and man through the receiving of divine knowledge.

The voice of God can represent an intimate knowledge of God, and this intimate knowledge of God destroys all your fears and distress. As David watched the display of a thunderstorm and wrote these words: "The voice of the Lord divides the flames of fire." He may have been dwelling on one of the many stresses he was feeling as a king and then looked up, saw the flash of lightning and then hearing the thunder, he could very well have been reminded that he was intimate with a powerful God who could destroy the lightning of his fear and distress.

Have you ever sat out under a porch roof during a thunderstorm? There is something very uplifting about a thunderstorm. For one thing, I have read where there is a release of ozone, which causes a chemical reaction in the human body to create a very positive or euphoric feeling. Couple that with a picture of the power of God's voice overpowering your fears and distresses and you have God sending you a special message. A message that He has everything under control. He will fight for you.

BEYOND THE LOOKING GLASS

I spend about three to four hours a day studying God's Word in the original Hebrew, Aramaic, and Greek. I usually write up my conclusions in a little word study or devotional that I send out to former students on a daily basis and also post on my website. Sometimes these studies follow a storyline where I travel behind a *Looking Glass* similar to Lewis Carroll's, *Through the Looking Glass.* In my office I have a four-foot high Daleth and hanging from the Daleth is a mirror. Similar to the story by Lewis Carroll, as I pass through this mirror I enter an alternative world filled with literary nonsense. In this world, I meet Hebrew letters which take on a certain personality and I experience various adventures with them where they instruct me in the meaning behind the letters and how they would apply to the particular verse that I am studying.

Study #3

Psalm 119:130: "The *entrance* of Your *words* gives light; it gives *understanding* to the simple."

I just hung up the phone. I knew I had to make a very important financial decision. My mind was filled with thoughts of how this decision would affect my life in this world, the pleasures and joys I experience in this world. However, I know I could not and must not make my decision without first consulting my Hebrew friend Byin (understanding, discernment) בִּין and I knew one place where Byin (understanding) בִּין lived and that is in Psalm 119:130. So, I quickly turned to this passage in my Hebrew Bible, but to my amazement, I discovered that Byin (understanding) בִּין along with his old pal Patach (entrance) פֶּתַח were missing. I was pretty sure I knew where to find Patach (entrance) פֶּתַח if he were missing and I figured I would also find Byin (understanding) בִּין in the same place hanging out with him.

I went to my office where I kept my Daleth with my *Looking Glass* hanging from it. Sure enough, there was Patach (entrance) פֶּתַח standing guard at the entrance to my *Looking Glass* hanging from my Daleth. "Patach," I said, "I sure do not understand why they made you the gatekeeper to my *Looking Glass.* "Maybe" replied Patach (entrance) פְּתַח, "Because that is what my name means, opening a gateway or portal. Perhaps your lack of understanding is because you have not consulted with Byin (understanding) בִּין." "Tell me something I don't know, like where in the blazes I can find him. I tell you I can never find Byin (understanding) בִּין when I need him. I confront Patach (entrance) פְּתַח and say, "You have any idea where he is, I was hoping to find him with you?" I tell my little friend, "I really need Byin (understanding) בִּין right now for an important decision I have to make." "Well," responded Patach (entrance) פְּתַח, "Byin (understanding) בִּין would not do you much good without God's Devar (words from the heart) דָּבָר, and if you haven't notice God's Devar (words from the heart) דָּבָר has also gone missing from Psalms 119:130. Byin (understanding) בִּין and

I knew you would be looking for God's Devar (words from the heart) דבר so Byin (understanding) בין has gone behind the *Looking Glass* to look for him. Do you care to step behind the *Looking Glass* and looked for God's Devar (words from the heart) דבר yourself?" Patach (entrance) פתח was right. I had not noticed that God's Devar (words from the heart) דבר had also gone missing because I was so focused on what Byin (understanding) בין had to say, but without God's Devar (words from the heart) דבר Byin (understanding) בין would have nothing to say.

I considered the letters of God's Devar (words from the heart) דבר Daleth ד, Beth ב, Resh ר. I recalled how the sages used to say that when you meet Daleth ד, it will ask you to examine the true nature of wealth. The Beth ב represents my heart and the resh ר represent the wholeness or what the heart will be filled with. It is what the heart could be filled with that becomes the issue. The Resh ר also represents a filling of the Holy Spirit, or in its shadow be a filling of sin, a filling of fleshly desires for the pleasures of this world which could chock off the Byin (understanding) בין of God's Devar (words from the heart) דבר.

I began my journey through the *Looking Glass* and found myself in a very delightful world. Well, of course, it was a delightful world, there was a big sign to the entrance of the playground of this world saying: "Chaim Bentorah's Playground." I saw the Daleth ד to God's Devar (words from the heart) דבר standing at the entrance to my playground. Daleth looked at me as if to say: "Is this what you believe wealth is?" He then opened the gate to the Beth (my heart) ב and the Resh ר (filling one's heart) who started to show Beth (my heart) ב around. He let Beth (my heart) ב climb up this huge statute. With great joy I saw that it was a statute of me. My oh my but I did indeed look impressive. Oh, what a glorious figure I was cut out to be with one hand on my lapel, another raised to heaven and my face with the look of a saint. Surely I bore the look of a very holy person. Why I must remember to call the Vatican as they would most certainly want to use my picture to model for a holy card. Then I looked around at all the delights in my playground for which Beth ב (my heart) had to enjoy and there was my old faithful Resh ר filling Beth (my heart) ב with them.

I notice a swing set that had seats shaped like burgers held in place by a chain of fries, Oh, how Beth (my heart) ב would love that. There were little spinners with handgrips that spin around in a circle. The round spinners were copper colored pennies. I know such a humble person as I would have no need for silver or gold but the value these copper spinners would more than delight Beth (my heart) ב. I could not help but notice the prize amusement in my park. There in the center was a sliding board made up of papers and pages of all my writings and books. Oh, yes, I know my Beth (my heart) ב would just love that. Behind all the playground equipment are hiking trails. I wondered if Beth (my heart) ב would like to take a hike. But then I noticed all those worry trees and fretting bushes ready to attack and made special note to advise my Beth (my heart) ב to avoid taking any hikes into the unknown, best just stay where it is safe.

Suddenly I hear an argument outside the gate to my playground. I look over to see that it was Byin (understanding) בין the word I had been looking for. I see Byin (understanding) בין (Beth ב, Yod י, Nun נ having an argument with the Daleth ד and Resh ר from God's Devar (words from the heart) דבר. The Beth ב (my heart) from Debar was off playing in my playground. I approached and asked if I could be of assistance. The Beth from Byin (understanding) בין turned toward me and pointed his finger at me saying: "You bet your big bibbie you can help." I wonder if his use of so many "b's" (Beth) was meant to be sarcastic. "Listen" says Byin (understanding) בין very firmly: "We came here at your request because you needed us Byin (understanding) בין. I brought with me my other two letters the Yod י who is a messenger from heaven and the Nun נ which is your faith so I can give you some understanding of the message from God's Devar (words from the heart) דבר, the Word of God. So what does the Daleth ד and Resh ר of Debar do? They tell their middle letter, the Beth ב (your heart) to go and run wild in your playground. So instead of the Beth (your heart) ב being filled with the Resh ר, (the Holy Spirit, repentance) Resh's shadow comes along and starts to fill the Beth (your heart) ב with all these other delights and we cannot even begin to give you an understanding of God's Devar (words from the heart) דבר to help you in your decision because the central letter to God's Devar (words from the heart) דבר the Beth (your heart) ב is off playing around in your playground. You will now make a decision based on the best interest of your Playground.

Well, hearing that I marched right into my playground and grabbed my Beth (my heart) ב by the ear, and dragged him kicking and screaming out of the playground and deposited him right in the center of God's Devar (words from the heart) דבר between the Daleth ד and the Resh ר where he belonged. I then declare; "Ok, now all of us are going to go back through my *Looking Glass* and you will assume your rightful place in Psalm 119:130. As we passed through my *Looking Glass* I reached out and grabbed Patach (entrance) פתח and dragged him with me tossing him back into my Hebrew Bible as well.

Once everyone is in their proper place I again look at these words and read. "The Patach or opening of the portal to your Devar or the Word of God in your heart which is filled with the Spirit of God will give you light and understanding (a message from heaven through the Holy Spirit)." However, if you allow your heart to play with all the things that are not of God, you will not be able to hear what Byin (understand) בין is saying.

CONCLUSION

CONCLUSION

I recall hearing the story of a woman who met a man at a party. She was attracted to him, but when he said he was a science fiction writer, she lost interest. She not only hated science fiction, but she also did not feel a writer was a very good prospect for a future relationship. However, this writer was persistent, and before long they were dating and then engaged to get married. The night this woman was engaged she sat up in bed pondering this man that she had fallen in love with and wondered just how much she knew of this man. She wished there was some way she could just get to know his inner thoughts and his heart. Suddenly she realized she had a copy of his book that she never read. She went to her bookcase, dusted off the cover and began to read his science fiction book. She not only read the entire book that night, but she also read through the book every night for the next few days.

Now, did I not say that this woman hated science fiction? Just what would prompt her to lose a night of sleep reading a science fiction book, and not only that but to re-read the book every night for the following days? The answer is simple, she fell in love with its author.

The reason so many Christians do not read their Bibles is because they have not really fallen in love with its author, but how can you fall in love with someone that you do not know? The only way to know and understand Him is through His Book that He has written for us.

Another reason people do not study the Bible is that they feel it is too difficult to read. They tell me that I am a Bible teacher who has taught Greek and Hebrew so naturally I will understand what I read, but they are just uneducated, and nothing in the Bible makes sense. My response to that is that I have studied the Bible for thirty-five years in the biblical languages and there is much that does not make sense to me as well. However, that does not keep me from studying the Bible, in fact, that is the very reason I began to study the Biblical languages.

There is another story of a salesman who paid a visit to a client who was a florist. As the salesman sat in the florist office waiting for his client to gather some papers together, he examined his bookshelf. On the shelf was one very thick book, the size of a dictionary, and it had one name for the title, *Roses*. The salesman said out loud, "How could anyone write so much about one flower?" Without missing a beat, the florist instructed the salesman to read the first line in the first chapter. He did, and in that one sentence we find the secret to understanding and studying the Word of God. It said; "If you love it enough, it will reveal its secrets."

Again, I am brought back to the key to studying the Word of God, if you love Him enough, you will have no problem spending four, five hours or more a day studying His Word and if you do love Him enough, He will reveal His secrets to you in his Word.

What I am offering in this book is meant for those who love God enough but cannot seem to go any further in the depth of their study than referencing a commentary or lexicon. If you love the Lord God with all their heart, soul and might, I am offering a tool that will allow you to go deeper into His Word. A tool which will take you just a little bit further after having completed a technical study of a verse or Hebrew word. It is a tool that will challenge you to take the next step and put that verse or word into an emotional context and then to meditate on it and allow the Holy Spirit to do His revelatory work and give you a personal message from God.

Is there a Divine design within the Hebrew language? Did God really put a built in commentary in each Hebrew word which can be decoded by using the meanings behind the Hebrew letters? Did God design the Hebrew language to bear all these associations and relationships to similar words and structures? Did God build into each word a numerical value that would correspond to other words with the same numerical value to give a person a deeper understanding of His Word? Maybe so, may not. Maybe these are all just coincidences as many liberal scholars would like us to believe. I find that when I pray and place my faith in God, coincidences happen, when I stop praying and stop believing, coincidences stop happening. Just given the benefit of the doubt that this manual is only presenting something that can be answered by coincidences, the discoveries of these coincidences will still help you find a deeper and more satisfying relationship with God and a hunger to study and read His word.

Christian families struggle with having a family devotional time which rarely amounts to nothing more than one parent doing all the talking or teaching. If families could take just one passage of Scripture and examine each word esoterically, it could be like a game, as it was in the Middle Ages, with each family member trying to unlock the right combination of meanings and numerical associations.

As to the question of whether the esoteric structure of the Hebrew Alphabet is of Divine design or the creation of man, that is a question to which we will never find a conclusive answer. However, one thing is certain, these coincidences do turn one's attention to the Word of God, and that cannot be such a bad thing.

Is there is a danger in taking the Gematria and meaning behind Hebrew letters too seriously? There is indeed, just as there is a danger in taking any study tool too seriously. There is an old story in the Talmud of a rabbi who took three students into Sod (the deep mysteries of God). In the end, one student died, one lost his faith and the other went insane. Only the rabbi who had the purest heart returned from the journey unharmed.

As a Bible College teacher, I have had students seek the deep mysteries of God without a pure heart. One was convinced that to get answer to prayer all he had to do was follow a certain formula he felt he discovered in the Bible. When his prayers went unanswered he lost his faith, left the ministry and has not returned to his former faith. I had another student who sought the mysteries of God. He studied day and night and became convinced that there was some inherent power in invoking the Hebrew name of God, YHWH. He soon reached the point believing that anyone who did not use the Hebrew name of God YHWH or the Hebrew name of Jesus, Yeshua, was not a true believer, and would go to hell. Before long he became convinced that only he and a small group of followers who thought he had the real truth and all of Christendom were deceived by Satan and doomed to hell. Many consider this former student of mine to be insane and considering his delusions of grandeur even I questioned his sanity. Then I had another student who, through his study of the Word of God became convinced God called him to enter a dangerous situation, totally ill equipped, and untrained. He went, only believing that the angels would protect him. Against all advice, he took what he felt was a step of faith and ended up losing his life. Just as the rabbi lost his three students to a loss of faith, insanity, and death, the same can easily happen if we enter into any form of biblical study without a pure heart and motives.

What I have presented is considered by some as mysticism, because they claim its origins are with Jewish mystics. However, if they study Jewish mystics, they would discover that in the true sense a Jewish mystic is only a person seeking a relationship with an unseen God. If that makes me a mystic, so I am.

I do not believe there is any inherent power in the Hebrew letters, but I do believe there is a power in the Word of God, the Bible. I offer nothing more than the *Old Time Religion* which was good enough for my fathers and it is good enough for me. I simply want to find ways to swim in some deeper waters and discover the treasures that my fathers did not have the tools at their disposal, that I have today with modern technology to use to make these discoveries.

Chaim Bentorah is the pseudonym of a Gentile Christian who taught college-level Biblical Hebrew and is an Amazon Bestselling Author. He prepared his students to take the placement exams for graduate school. He has now developed a method of study where he can prepare any Believer, regardless of age or academic background, to study the Word of God using Biblical Hebrew.

Chaim Bentorah received his B.A. degree from Moody Bible Institute in Jewish Studies and his M.A. degree from Denver Seminary in Old Testament and Hebrew and his PhD in Biblical Archeology. His Doctoral Dissertation was on the "Esoteric Structure of the Hebrew Alphabet." He has taught Classical Hebrew at World Harvest Bible College for thirteen years and also taught Hebrew for three years as a language course for Christian Center High School. He is presently teaching Biblical Hebrew and Greek to pastors in the Metro Chicago area.

www.chaimbentorah.com

Other books by Chaim Bentorah

Hebrew Word Study: Revealing The Heart Of God

Journey into Silence: Transformation Through Contemplation, Wonder, and Worship

For Whom My Soul Loves: A Hebrew Teacher's Journey to Understanding God's Love

God's Love for Us: A Hebrew Teacher Explores the Heart of God through the Marriage Relationship

Hebrew Word Study: Ancient Biblical Words Put into a Modern Context with the Help of the People Who Ride My Bus

Is This Really Revival?

Biblical Truths From Uncle Otto's Farm

Made in United States
Orlando, FL
16 October 2023